A True Story

A Swan Family's Amazing Journey

BRONWYN GABY

To order additional copies of this book, contact:
Xlibris
1-800-455-039
www.xlibris.com.au
Orders@Xlibris.com.au

In a suburb near a big city, there is a very big, beautiful park called Mawson Park. It has two different adventure playgrounds, one for big kids and one for younger ones. It has a sports oval, a cycle track and lots of trees. It is a good place to have a barbecue or a birthday party.

Right in the middle of the park is a billabong, a small pond with a very small island in the middle. The council built a double fence around the outside of the pond to keep people away from the little island so that ducks and other birds could go there to lay eggs and to be safe.

Although many birds have made this park their home, it is not always very safe. There is not enough food to feed *all* the baby birds that are born here. A mother duck has to be very careful to protect her ducklings from cats, crows, snakes and kookaburras. There are dangers all around!

One day two swans flew down to the small pond and noticed the little island right in the middle. What a good spot to lay their eggs and wait for them to hatch!

Soon five small grey cygnets broke out of the eggs. That was a lot for the two parents to look after!

Even though they were very tiny, the baby swans had to leave the safety of the island and look for food. They had just been born, but they swam in the water and then scrambled out onto the grass to eat seeds and plants.

It was the school holidays, and hundreds of people were at the park. They loved to see the cygnets, but when people came too close, the male swan got frightened.

He flapped his wings to make himself seem very big, and the mother swan called her babies to come very close to her. They hid under her wings, as close to each other as they could get.

To escape from the people and all the noise, the swans tried to get back to the water, but they couldn't find a way through the fence. The cygnets could fit through but not the adult swans.

The male swan soon realised that this was *not* a very good park to bring up his babies! He set off flying all around the suburb, looking for a bigger and safer park with a lot more water. And looking down, he found a perfect place.

But it was far, far away.

What could he do? How was he going to get his family to this much bigger and safer lake? The cygnets couldn't fly. They had only just been born, so how could they walk all the way to this new place?

Nevertheless, the only solution was to try.

Early one morning the family of seven set off. They walked slowly across the park, through the trees, and over the oval. Then they reached a road that went up a steep hill.

There were houses on each side of the road, and the only food the swans could eat were seeds and grass on people's front lawns. Halfway up the hill, the five cygnets were too tired to go on.

Two children in a house were very surprised to look out of their window and see a whole family of seven swans resting under a bush in their front garden.

The next day, very early in the morning, the family of swans set off again. Morning joggers and people walking their dogs saw them and wondered where they were going.

How could such tiny cygnets possibly keep walking?

And what about the crows that flew close by? They were sure a baby swan would make a tasty meal!

At the end of the day, they still were making their way up the hill, walking slowly, and going from garden to garden.

The swan family spent another night hiding under a bush, with the babies as close to the parents as they could be.

That night a cat tried to sneak up and steal away a baby swan, but the male swan stretched out his feathers and flapped his wings and looked as scary as he could.

The cat changed his mind and ran away!

Finally they arrived at the edge of the new park. They were close but not close enough.

They still had to walk a long way to the water, and there were new dangers to face. One of the cygnets was so tired that one of the adults gave it a ride.

This was a park where people could walk their dogs. Many large dogs were running around, and the swans and their babies were in a lot of danger.

One lady who was walking her dogs saw them. She understood where they were trying to go, so she decided to help them.

As the swans slowly made their way through the park, she followed behind them, making sure other dogs kept away.

Finally the family arrived at the lake the male swan had seen from the air. And it was everything he had hoped for! There were reeds to hide in and a lot of food in the water and on the grass. And most amazing of all was that all five cygnets had survived the journey.

Could the cygnets now rest and grow into swans?

Cygnets take many months to become adult swans. They start off looking nothing like swans.

They are grey and small and have thin fuzz instead of feathers. Perhaps they do look a little like ugly ducklings when they are young.

Gradually their necks stretch out, and their bodies get bigger. Then amongst the grey down, black feathers begin to grow. The young swans start flapping small, stubby wings, building up muscles that will help them to fly when all their feathers have appeared.

It is not often that a whole family of five cygnets can make it into adults. Danger is present every day until the swans are big enough to fight back.

But this family survived because of the care of both parents and the help they received from the people along the way.

And a lot of luck always helps.

The swans stayed at the lake for a very long time, eating, swimming, and growing strong.

One day the people who had been keeping an eye on them realised all seven swans had flown away.

Would any of them return one day with a new family? Maybe!

Printed in the United States
By Bookmasters